RUNAWAY RUNES

SHORT

GROOKS

I

PIET HEIN

40 books among which are

GRUK, ESPERANTO ELDONO

GRUK FRA ALLE ÅRENE 1

300 gruk, 1940 — 1964

GRUK FRA ALLE ÅRENE 2

300 gruk til 1940 — 1964

GROOKS I

GROOKS II

GROOKS III

GROOKS IV

GROOKS V

I FOLKEMUNDE, korte gruk I

DET KRAFTENS ORD, korte gruk II

RUNAWAY RUNES, Short grooks 1

GROOKS IN MUSIC

DIGTE FRA ALLE ÅRENE

PIET
HEIN

RUNAWAY RUNES

SHORT
GROOKS
I

With the assistance of Jens Arup

BORGENS POCKETBOOKS 94

© 1968 ASPILA S.A.

Cover and illustration PIET HEIN

Printing: Antikva Offset A/S, Herlev, Denmark

ISBN 87 418 2620 5

Third edition 1973

Taking fun as simply fun
and earnestness in earnest
shows how thoroughly thou none
of the two discernest.

If a nasty jagged stone
  gets into your shoe,
thank the Lord it came alone -
  what if it were two.

Mind these three:
  T. T. T.
Hear their chime:
  Things Take Time.

Losing one glove is certainly painful
but nothing compared to the pain
of losing one, throwing away the other,
and finding the first one again.

Problems worthy
of attack
prove their worth
by hitting back.

Nature, our father and mother,
    gave us all we have got.
The state, our elder brother,
    swipes the lot.

To be brave is to behave
  bravely when your heart is faint.
So you can be really brave
  only when you really ain't.

If they made diving boards
  six inches shorter —
think how much sooner
  you'd be in the water.

Man's a kind
  of Missing Link
fondly thinking
  he can think.

Naive you are:
if you believe
life favours those
who aren't naive.

*Small people often overrate
the charm of being tall
which is that you appreciate
the charm of being small.*

Anxieties yield
    at a negative rate,
increasing in smallness
    the longer they wait.

The noble art of losing face
    may one day save the human race
and turn into eternal merit
    what weaker minds would call disgrace.

The only defence
  that is more than pretence
is to act on the fact
  that there is no defence.

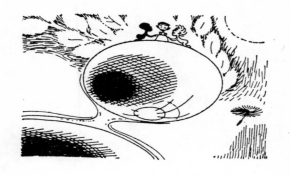

Co-
existence
or no
existence.

Men, said the Devil,
   are good to their brothers:
they don't want to mend
   their own ways but each others.

When people always try to take
    the very smallest piece of cake
how can it also always be
    that that's the one that's left for me?

When you're adding up committees
 there's a useful rule of thumb:
that talents make a difference
 but follies make a sum.

If no thought
   your mind does visit
make your speech
   not too explicit.

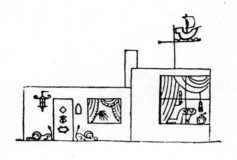

You'll conquer the present
   suspiciously fast
if you smell of the future
   and stink of the past.

As pastor X steps out of bed
  he slips a neat disguise on:
that halo round his priestly head
  is really his horizon.

He that lets
the small things find him
leaves the great
undone behind him.

We shall have to evolve
  problem solvers galore —
since each problem we solve
  creates ten problems more.

The road to wisdom? — Well, it's plain
   and simple to express:
Err and err and err again
   but less and less and less.

The human spirit sublimates
the impulses it thwarts;
a healthy sex life mitigates
the lust for other sports.

Love is like
    a pineapple
sweet and
    undefineable.

The soul may be a mere pretence,
the mind makes very little sense.
So let us value the appeal
of that which we can taste and feel.

I love excess
of fruitfulness.
Let other fools
pay more for less.

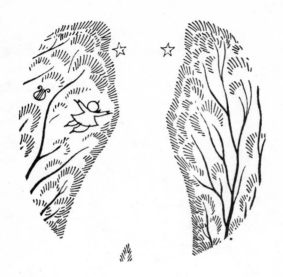

Love while you've got
love to give.
Live while you've got
life to live.

Stomach-ache can be a curse;
heart-ache may be even worse:
so thank Heaven on your knees
if you've got but one of these.

Everything's either
concave or -vex,
so whatever you dream
will be something with sex.

Of drink and victuals
   and suchlike stuff
a bit too little
   is just enough.

Life makes sense,
   and who could doubt it,
if we have
   no doubt about it.

My old clock used to tell the time
  and subdivide diurnity;
but now it's lost both hands and chime
  and only tells eternity.

There's an art in knowing when.
   Never try to guess.
Toast until it smokes and then
   twenty seconds less.

Here lies, extinguished in his prime,
  a victim of modernity:
but yesterday he had no time —
  and now he has eternity.

Double-doors are justified
 because they're comfortably wide.
Therefore we only half undo 'em.
 and therefore nothing can get thru 'em.

To make a name for learning
   when other roads are barred,
take something very easy
   and make it very hard.

Experts have
  their expert fun
telling us
    things can't be done.

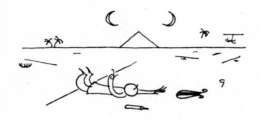

Our choicest plans have fallen through,
    our airiest castles tumbled over,
because of lines we neatly drew
    and later neatly stumbled over.

Our so-called limitations, I believe,
   apply to faculties we don't apply.
We don't discover what we can't achieve
   until we make an effort not to try.

Idiots, are really
one hundred per cent
when they are also
intelligent.

Knowing what
    thou knowest not
is in a sense
    omniscience.

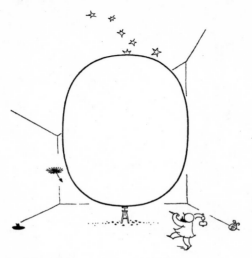

There is one art,
  no more, no less:
to do all things
  with artlessness.

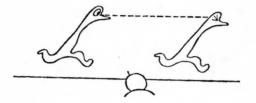

He who aims
to keep abreast
is for ever
second best.

Sub specie
  aeternitatis
even the dearest bought
  is gratis.

A lifetime is more
than sufficiently long
for people to get
what there is of it wrong.

Living is
    a thing you do
now or never —
    which do you?

As eternity
is reckoned
there's a lifetime
in a second.

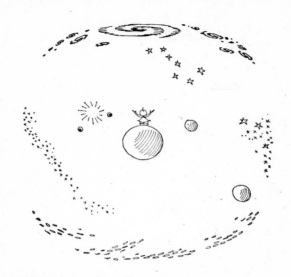

The universe may
    be as great as they say.
But it wouldn't be missed
    if it didn't exist.

He on whom
 God's light does fall
sees the great things
 in the small.

Smile a while
    ere day is done
and all your gall
    will soon be gone.

Shun advice
  at any price.
That's what I
  call good advice.